¹/₁₇

Helen Keller

Kitson Jazynka

NATIONAL GEOGRAPHIC

Washington, D.C.

For kids who believe life is an adventure,
like Helen Keller did —K. J.

Trade paperback ISBN: 978-1-4263-2669-1
Reinforced library binding ISBN: 978-1-4263-2670-7

The publisher and author gratefully acknowledge the expert content review of this book by Beth A. Haller, Ph.D., professor of journalism/new media at Towson University and editor of *Byline of Hope: Collected Newspaper and Magazine Writing of Helen Keller*, the review for sensitivity and inclusive language by the Mid-Atlantic ADA Center, and the literacy review of this book by Mariam Jean Dreher, professor of reading education, University of Maryland, College Park.

Photo Credits

Cover (LO), Bettmann/Getty Images; cover (background), Mary Terriberry/Shutterstock; 1 (CTR), Granger.com — All rights reserved; 3 (LO RT), Oscar White/Corbis Historical/Getty Images; 5 (CTR), New York Times Co./Getty Images; 6 (CTR), Bettman/Getty Images; 6 (LO), GraphicaArtis/Getty Images; 7 (LO RT), Keystone-France/Getty Images; 9 (UP), The George F. Landegger Collection of Alabama Photographs in Carol M. Highsmith's America, Library of Congress, Prints and Photographs Division; 9 (LO), Buyenlarge/Getty Images; 10 (UP), Bettmann/Getty Images; 11 (LO), Buyenlarge/Getty Images; 12 (CTR), Ray Hems/Shutterstock; 12 (LO), spxChrome/Shutterstock; 13 (UP), IMAGEPAST/Alamy Stock Photo; 13 (CTR), Ahmad Faizal Yahy/Shutterstock; 13 (LO), UniversalImagesGroup/Getty Images; 14 (LO), Sandra van der Steen/Shutterstock; 15 (UP), Bettmann/Getty Images; 16 (CTR), From The Brewster Historical Society Archives, 2015.1.1; 17 (CTR), Miracle Worker 2010/Universal History Archive/UIG/Bridgeman Images; 18 (LO), Africa Studio/Shutterstock; 19 (UP), Bettmann/Getty Images; 20 (UP), Bettmann/Getty Images; 20 (CTR), Library of Congress Prints and Photographs Division; 20 (CTR), Agency Animal Picture/Getty Images; 21 (UP RT), Larry Burrows/Getty Images; 21 (CTR LE), Bettmann/Getty Images; 21 (CTR RT), George Rinhart/Getty Images; 21 (LO), PhotoQuest/Getty Images; 22 (LO), George Grantham Bain/Getty Images; 23 (UP), Topical Press Agency/Getty Images; 25 (UP), FPG/Archive Photos/Getty Images; 25 (CTR), Bettmann/Getty Images; 26 (UP), Keystone-France/Getty Images; 27 (LO LE), Bettmann/Getty Images; 28 (CTR), Christina Ascani; 29 (LO), Library of Congress Prints and Photographs Division; 30 (UP RT), NG Maps; 30 (CTR LE), From The Brewster Historical Society Archives, 2015.1.1; 30 (LO RT), Bettmann/Getty Images; 31 (UP LE), Africa Studio/Shutterstock; 31 (CTR LE), Buyenlarge/Getty Images; 31 (CTR RT), PhotoQuest/Getty Images; 31 (LO RT), Fred Stein Archive/Getty Images; 32 (UP LE), John Birdsall/Alamy Stock Photo; 32 (UP RT), Axsimen/Shutterstock; 32 (CTR LE), Ninell/Shutterstock; 32 (CTR RT), Hannah Peters/Getty Images; 32 (LO RT), Bettmann/Getty Images; 24-25 (LO), komkrit Preechachanwate/Shutterstock; 32 (LO LE), Sandra van der Steen/Shutterstock; HEADER (throughout), Visual Cortex/Shutterstock; VOCAB (throughout), Kary Nieuwenhuis/Getty Images

National Geographic supports K–12 educators with ELA Common Core Resources. Visit natgeoed.org/commoncore for more information.

Table of Contents

Who Was Helen Keller?

Close your eyes and cover your ears with your hands. It's dark and quiet. Can you imagine living in such a world?

Helen Keller lived like that. She was blind and deaf. But she didn't let that stop her from learning as much as she could. She used what she learned to help other blind or deaf people have better lives.

Words to Know

BLIND: Unable to see

DEAF: Unable to hear

Helen Keller is featured on the Alabama state quarter.

Keller (left) often traveled with her assistant, Polly Thomson.

In Her Own Words

"Life is either a daring adventure or nothing."

In Keller's time, disabled people were often ignored or sent to live away from their families. Keller worked to change how others thought about disabled people. She wrote articles and books. She traveled the world and spoke out. She inspired disabled people with her courage. She helped change unfair treatment for other people, too.

Words to Know

DISABLED: Having a condition that limits a person's ability to do something as others do

Growing Up

Keller was born on June 27, 1880. She lived with her family in Tuscumbia, Alabama, U.S.A. When she was about a year and a half old, she got sick with a high fever. Soon she felt better. But she didn't blink when the sun shone in her face. She couldn't hear the dinner bell ring. Doctors said she had lost her sight and hearing forever.

That's a FACT!

You can visit Keller's childhood home, Ivy Green, in Tuscumbia, Alabama.

This is the home where Keller grew up.

Keller at age seven

For young Keller, the world had become dark, soundless, and confusing. Most children learn to speak by hearing and watching others. Keller could do neither. When she tried to speak, no one could understand.

She must have felt lonely and frustrated. She kicked and threw things. Her parents were frustrated, too. But they wouldn't give up on their smart, spirited daughter.

At Ivy Green, actors perform *The Miracle Worker*, a play about Keller's life.

In Her Time

When Keller was a girl in the 1880s, many things were different from how they are today.

TRANSPORTATION: People often traveled by train, steamboat, or wagons pulled by horses or oxen.

HOME LIFE: Families heated their homes with wood fires. They pumped water for the house from an outdoor well.

U.S. EVENTS: When Grover Cleveland became president of the United States in 1885, women did not have the right to vote.

FOOD: Few people shopped in stores for food. Instead they raised farm animals. They also grew fruits and vegetables to feed their families.

SCHOOL: Children were taught at home or in one-room schoolhouses. Children of wealthy families might attend boarding schools.

Learning Letters and Words

A few years later, Keller's mother read about a school for blind and deaf children. There, students learned how to finger-spell words into a person's hands. She wondered if her little girl could learn, too.

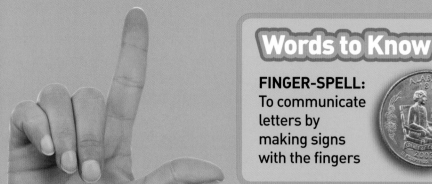

Words to Know

FINGER-SPELL: To communicate letters by making signs with the fingers

This is how to finger-spell the letter *L*. In Keller's time, a blind and deaf person would touch the sign to read it.

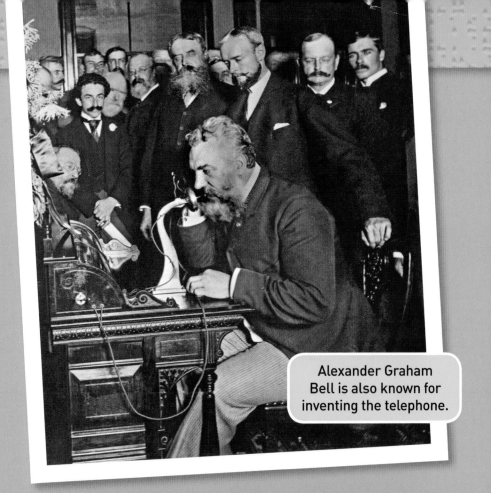

Alexander Graham Bell is also known for inventing the telephone.

Keller and her parents visited Alexander Graham Bell in Washington, D.C. He was well known for teaching deaf children. Bell helped the Kellers find a teacher for their daughter.

That teacher was Annie Sullivan. She arrived when Keller was six years old. Sullivan finger-spelled words into her student's hand. But Keller didn't understand.

Keller and her teacher, Annie Sullivan

Annie Sullivan

Annie Sullivan was 20 years old when she came to live with the Kellers on March 3, 1887. She was partly blind, and she had gone to a school for the blind in Massachusetts, U.S.A. She was smart and stubborn, just like Keller.

The pair worked together for 49 years. Because of her success in helping Keller, Sullivan was called a miracle worker.

Actors show Sullivan pumping water into Keller's hands.

One day, Sullivan finger-spelled "w-a-t-e-r." At the same time, she pumped water onto Keller's other hand. Suddenly Keller understood that the liquid she felt had a name and that Sullivan was spelling it. She danced for joy. She learned 30 more words before bedtime.

Keller couldn't wait to learn more. Within a year, she knew more than 900 words. She mastered braille and typing by age 10. Later she attended high school in New York City. Sullivan went with Keller and finger-spelled for her.

Words to Know

BRAILLE: A reading system with raised dots that stand for letters and numbers

a person reading braille

Keller graduated from Radcliffe College in 1904.

At the time, few disabled people went to college. But Keller did. She insisted on the same treatment as other students. With Sullivan's help, she read books and wrote papers.

7 COOL FACTS
About
Helen Keller

1 With Sullivan's help, Keller learned by doing— she rode horses, went swimming and sledding, and touched tadpoles.

In college, Keller learned to read and write French, German, and Latin.

2

3 Keller had a keen sense of vibrations around her and could identify people and pets by their footsteps.

Keller had a special pocket watch with braille features on the outside to tell time with her hands.

4

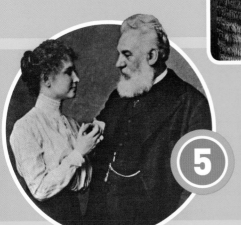

5

Keller and Alexander Graham Bell became lifelong friends.

Keller never saw her own face in a mirror.

6

7

Keller wrote 12 books, as well as many articles for well-known newspapers and magazines.

Finding Her Voice

By now, many people had heard about Keller. She was the young blind and deaf woman who could read and write. She used her growing fame to help others understand the lives of disabled people. Through writing, she shared her ideas about equal treatment.

In Her Own Words

"One can never consent to creep when one feels an impulse to soar."

But writing and finger-spelling were sometimes too slow for Keller. She wanted to use her voice to speak about change.

Helen practiced speaking. In 1909, she got help from a singing teacher. A few years later, she was able to give her first speech. She kept practicing. She gave more speeches.

She spoke up not only for disabled people, but also for children and the poor. As a suffragette (suf-rih-JET), she spoke up for women, too.

Words to Know

SUFFRAGETTE: A woman who works for the right of women to vote

1880
Born on June 27 in Tuscumbia, Alabama

1882
Suffers an illness that leaves her blind and deaf

1887
Begins work with teacher Annie Sullivan

That's a FACT! Between 1946 and 1957, Keller spoke in 35 countries on five continents.

1894
Attends a school for the deaf in New York City

1902
Publishes her first book, *The Story of My Life*

1903
Visits the White House to meet with President Teddy Roosevelt

Keller reads a book in braille to a group of blind children.

In 1924, Keller began working for the American Foundation for the Blind. She raised money that was used to help blind people get education and jobs.

1904
Graduates from Radcliffe College in Cambridge, Massachusetts

1920
The 19th Amendment to the U.S. Constitution gives American women the right to vote

1924
Begins work with the American Foundation for the Blind

In the early 1930s, U.S. lawmakers were writing a new law to help disabled people. Keller pushed for the law to include the blind. She also worked to make braille the standard system of reading and writing for blind people.

That's a FACT!

When Keller met President Dwight Eisenhower in 1953, she touched his face to "see" his smile.

Remembering Helen Keller

A statue of Keller stands in the Capitol Building in Washington, D.C.

Keller spent her life helping others. Her words showed the world how much disabled people could learn and do. Her work changed many lives for the better.

Keller died at her home on June 1, 1968. She was almost 88 years old. She is remembered for her hard work trying to make the world a better place for everyone.

In Her Own Words

"The best and most beautiful things in the world cannot be seen or even touched—they must be felt with the heart."

QUIZ WHIZ

See how many questions you can get right!
Answers are at the bottom of page 31.

1

Where was Keller born?

A. Alabama
B. New York
C. Washington, D.C.
D. Massachusetts

2

How old was Keller when Annie Sullivan became her teacher?

A. six years old
B. ten years old
C. a year and a half old
D. twenty years old

What important event happened at the water pump?

A. Keller had a drink of water.
B. Keller showed her teacher how to pump water.
C. Keller filled a bucket with water.
D. Keller learned the meaning of the word "water."

3

4

Keller learned braille so she could _____.

A. help her mother with chores around the house
B. read
C. play outside
D. tie her shoes

In 1902, Keller wrote _____.

5

A. her first book, *The Story of My Life*
B. the story of Annie Sullivan's childhood
C. a famous letter to her parents
D. her first comic book

6

As a suffragette, Keller believed women should have the right to _____.

A. get an education
B. get married
C. vote
D. drive a car

How did Keller help disabled people?

7

A. She wrote about the lives of disabled people.
B. She gave speeches about equal treatment.
C. She raised money to help the blind.
D. She did all of the above.

BLIND: Unable to see

ALPHABET:

A B C D E F G H I
J K L M N O P Q R
S T U V W X Y Z

BRAILLE: A reading system with raised dots that stand for letters and numbers

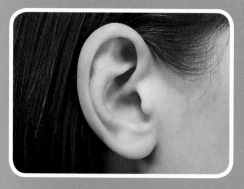

DEAF: Unable to hear

DISABLED: Having a condition that limits a person's ability to do something as others do

FINGER-SPELL: To communicate letters by making signs with the fingers

SUFFRAGETTE: A woman who works for the right of women to vote